PRESENTS

ALL ABOUT TAG TEAMS
FACT BOOK

BY LARRY HUMBER

CHECKERBOARD PRESS
NEW YORK

Some wrestlers like to go it alone. Others like company. In the pages to come, you are going to meet some of the World Wrestling Federation's top tag teams.

Let's get started with the fearsome Legion of Doom...

LEGION OF DOOM

✱ Legion of Doom is made up of Hawk and Animal. Who is who? Well, Hawk has less hair than Animal. A better way to tell them apart is the paint they wear on their faces. Animal has a spider painted on his forehead; Hawk doesn't.

* Hawk and Animal come from the city where Michael Jordan plays his basketball— Chicago.

* Hawk and Animal wear equipment usually associated with the sport of football—shoulder pads. But their pads are spiked.

✳ A crashing clothesline off the top ropes is Legion of Doom's best-known move. They call it the Doomsday Device. Few opponents have recovered from it.

✳ Hawk and Animal like to say, "Oh what a rush!"

✱ WWF Tag Team Champions the Nasty Boys are one of the Legion's main rivals. Like Legion, they are a very strong team.

✱ At *WrestleMania VII*, Hawk and Animal needed only minutes to put away Power and Glory with the Doomsday Device.

THE ROCKERS

* Shawn Michaels and Marty Jannetty are the Rockers. Shawn is the blond; Marty, the dark-haired one.

* The two Rockers weigh in at just over the 460-pound mark. That's about what Earthquake weighs all by himself.

* The Rockers are known for their exciting ring entrances and high-flying maneuvers.

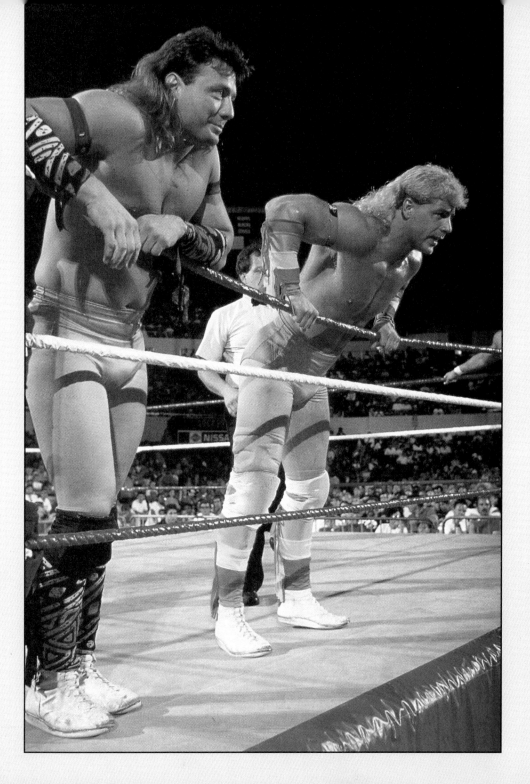

✱ Some say the Rockers cheat because often both are in the ring at the same time. But wrestlers are allowed five seconds to tag in and out, so the Rockers aren't breaking any rules.

✴ The Rockers share the interests of many young men. "We both like to chase girls and go out on the town," Marty says.

✴ Both Shawn and Marty are big music lovers. "We like to listen to our rock 'n' roll very loud all day and all night," Shawn says.

THE BUSHWHACKERS

* The Bushwhackers—Luke and Butch—come from a land down under, New Zealand.

✳ Luke and Butch are very fond of each other. They show their affection by licking each other's heads.

✳ They aren't known for their table manners. They like to eat right out of the can—especially if they are having sardines, one of their favorite foods.

✳ Those heads
have another
purpose. One of the
Bushwhackers' best
weapons is the
Bushwhacker
battering ram. One
of them grabs the
other by the head
and uses it to ram
an opponent.

✽ The Bushwhackers don't walk the way everybody else does. They like to swing their arms and kick up their legs, which they call power walking.

✳ Luke and Butch say they "want to see everybody do the Bushwhacker walk."

✳ The Bushwhackers made a surprise appearance at *WrestleMania VI.* Disguised as program sellers, they chased the Honky Tonk Man and Greg Valentine out of the ring. Then they destroyed their guitars.

THE NASTY BOYS

* As you can guess, the Nasty Boys—Brian Knobbs and Jerry Sags—are not nice guys. They like beating and bullying people.

✳ The Boys come from Allentown, Pennsylvania. It is one tough town.

✳ "We like to see the little piggies squeal," snarls Sags. He is the dark-haired one. He is missing a few teeth, too.

✱ "We get our fun putting on all the hurt in the world," says Knobbs. He is the blond.

* Knobbs and Sags are managed by Jimmy Hart, the Mouth of the South, who is arguably the most devious manager in the WWF.

* The Nasty Boys won the Tag Team Championship at *WrestleMania VII*. They defeated Jim Neidhart and Bret Hart, the Hart Foundation.

* The Boys won only by bashing Neidhart in the head with their manager's motorcycle helmet, knocking him out.

✳ From the Land of the Rising Sun—Japan—comes the Orient
Express. They even have a Japanese flag on their robes.

✳ The Express is made up of Kato and Tanaka. Kato is the one with the mask.

* Mr. Fuji manages the Express. He wears a bowler hat and carries a cane that he sometimes uses illegally to help his wrestlers in the ring.

* Mr. Fuji has taught Kato and Tanaka that the quickest way to win is to make your opponents suffer great pain.

* Both men can do more than wrestle. They are also martial arts experts.

✱ The Express knows the ways of the world. They say they want to dominate wrestling "the same way Japan dominates world finance."

✱ The Express met the Rockers at *WrestleMania VI*. They won, but not without some help from Mr. Fuji. He used his cane to trip Marty Jannetty.